THOUGHTS

Thoughts

Athena Ezra

Published by Athena Ezra, 2024.

While every precaution has been taken in the preparation of this book, the publisher assumes no responsibility for errors or omissions, or for damages resulting from the use of the information contained herein.

THOUGHTS

First edition. December 20, 2024.

Copyright © 2024 Athena Ezra.

ISBN: 979-8230020899

Written by Athena Ezra.

Table of Contents

To my Papa Sydric,

Thank you for inspiring me to live up on my dreams. Your death shocked me and yet your words of wisdom came up disturbing me every day and night.

"GO LIVE YOUR DREAMS"

I miss you everyday and you'll be in my heart forever.

Thanks Jessica for the beautiful book cover.

FINALLY

you were the start of my freedom,
yet you aren't meant for me,
I fought for you,
but still you aren't meant for me,
Then the breaking happen,
even I can't fixed
So I had to leave you,
with regrets,guilts and shame,
But isn't it ironic,
I thought you were the end of it all

FINALLY, Let go

Yet you aren't
Fear hold me back
to explore the other side,
grateful for my parents,
who knows me well enough,
to pick me up in pieces
to let go.
You were my greatest lesson
and my greatest what if but,
Now, I have let you go,
in my own way.

MOVING ON..

sun shining
might mistook it
for morning
yet its early in the evening
some are in the dreaming
mundane things
Felt extra extraordinary
i'd be happy to sing
something has change
the river knows it
flowing in on its edges
welcome it with a hit

GOODBYE

I love you,
I loved you,
I loved you,
But its time,
to forget about you.

WHEN

I often daydream
sweets dreams
of other people
but not you
I can quite figure you out yet
I have a thought of you,
Are you thinking of me too?
I will wait,
waiting for you to find me
Until then,
Be well and be good

HOW

How can I accept?
When there is no one making an offer.
How can I hold?
If there is no one who will lend a hand.
How can I be complete?
If deep inside, I felt something's missing.
How can I be happy?
If my thinking felt badly.

HOW can?

How can I be content?
If I want more.
How can I sacrifice?
If I have nothing to give up.
How can I trust?
If I experience betrayal.
How can I show love?
If nobody even dares to take it.
How can I be certain?
If I am still confused.

HOW could?

How could I be true?
If I am still holing on the past.
How could I share?
If no one seems to be interested.
How can I follow the rules?
If the rules are breaking my heart.
How could I move on?
If you keep giving me reason not to.
How can I forget you?
If I am still in love you.

WHAT

Sit with me,
And let me ponder.
Sip away your sorrows
Until the sun rises on the morrow.
A heart so fragile
That even life feel
So beguile
For all the things
I have done
My regrets,
Let it be gone.

WHERE

The Sea clouds me
There was a time
When I witnessed
The concoction of the clouds
And sea
I was the one in between
Them,
That alone was the,
Greatest love triangle
Of all time.

WHY

I hate you!
my heart aches
Why'd you leave?
without
saying goodbye.
I haven't
it hurts
more
talking to the wind
without someone responding
in my mourning.

THERE

I am gonna be there
But right now,
I am still here
So let's see
I am acting
Positively.

YOU

Learn to rest when your unrest
Let emotions go as it flows,
Be drawn but don't take too long,
Life is all about struggles,
It can get tangled but,
Try to loosen it's grip,
You will know on what to bet,
So smile and get up,
Because the world will be lonely,
Without you in it.

RAIN

Amidst the sandstorm,
rustling in the road,
A sprinkle of rain,
Washed away the blues,
I felt deep inside,
The longing of fresh brewed coffee,
seems so far,
Snap!
Reality is catching on.

SUMMER

Faded trees,
coming in as a tease
Steadying,
this unruly heart,
whilst shining so bright,
Bask in its sparkle,
and lead.

SPRING

Wondering what
feels right,
to let go,
so it might?
I can't,
I won't but
I must
a little drizzle
a little sunshine,
a season change
comes in presumably
Spring ain't it.
Flowers in full bloom,
downing its path
and so
Auf wiedersehen WINTER!

WINTER

My favorite
even though,
it hurts.
The cold
it brought
give some warmths
to many people
who forgot
the beauty
of being
human
which is
the gift of giving.

READY

Are you ready?
Are you sure?
This time
its a different you
Do I look ready?
My mind says, I am
but my heart contradicts
there on different sides
So I ain't ready yet
but you've been waiting for this
Some feelings stuck.
In my solitude, I am ready
In reality, I am a mess.

TRAUMA

I have learned to managed it little by little
but hurt tends to build up over time
Should I forgive myself?
not to put much pressure in myself?
I am not perfect
Yet this chaos keeps triggerring
Even if I do accept it,
Some logic doesn't make sense,
Understand it,
yet a part of you seems to be broken.

SOMETIMES

i wish I didn't know everything
I wish I am not that sensitive
it hurts me
it hurts you.
it's all in the head, they say
I wish I can just pick it up
throw it on the trash
and be done with it.

SOMEWHERE

Are you happy?
Fulfilled?
Content?
Safe?
I wish you do
I pray that you do
I hope that you are
I love you.

SOMEDAY

seeing you smile.
is making my heart beats fast,
it has been awhile,
since you had it,last.
You are amazing
Remember that,
You are the light
I've been waiting.

SOMETHING

I'm here,
Can't you see?
Dying,
Waiting,
Hoping,
Praying.
if its not your will,
Can you take it?
It will
hurt me less.

SOMETHING, to wait

I'll wait until
its ready
I'll wait till you say I'm ready.
I'm trusting you!
I'm surrendering in your name.
in jesus christ, amen.

SOMEHOW

I'll meet you,
I know I will,
I wish we can love freely
No more pain.
Understand me,
for my personality,
coz then
I'll love you forever.

DARK

I am a mess,
bawled out,
crumpled up,
hopeless.
Warfare in my mind
its getting real
and yet I hear, a thought.
Be still.

LOST

When I was lost,
I wept not
for the rejection,
I wept for the expectation.
My selfishness was so profound
that it was hard to fall,
I seek, complained on HIM,
I was angry
and put all the blame to HIM.

LIGHT

When my eyes bawled out,
i didn't hear anything
Secretly hoping for
a comfort.
I didn't ask for more,
It hurts but I know
I need to move on
I needed some light,
Someone,
Something,
Somewhere,
Now.

HIM

I found HIM
in my own way
it's difficult
still chasing HIM.
I am not worthy,
I am still sinning,
but I am willing to
ask for redemption.
FORGIVE ME
for not knowing more,
not trusting more,
not loving more.

MYSELF

Come find me,
Come rescue me,
I am at war
with myself.
I wish you are here
To hear my vicious thoughts,
I'm losing myself
Please, help me

LOOK AT ME

Look at me,
I'm not okay,
Look at me,
See the hurt in my eyes,
Look at me,
I'm drowning
Look at me,
Before I...

TO MY FUTURE

Hug me,
tightly.
Hug me
till it hurts
Hold me,
assure me,
be my security
I am safe on my own
but for you,
I'll melt
and give my all.
Come find me.
I'm still waiting.

STILL

Be still,
conjures a hint of rebellion
depth in my soul
that thrives in chaos
masking it with stoic calmness,
That's oblivious
to the ugly cries,
silent screams
that I, too
am not willing
to concede.

TRAVEL

I crave for eccentricity,
to counter my oblivion.
I crave for the journey,
Not much on the destination.

MOMENT

Just one,
one smile,
one hug,
one word,
one look
and then
Sayonara...

PRAY

Pray.
a thought,
a whisper,
a sigh,
So I kneeled,
cried,
and break.

HOME

I always have
But i flew away,
to chase my dreams,
So young,
So rebellious,
So kindred
and then life
threws a curveball,
broken wings,
broken heart,
broken spirit,
and someone says;
COME HOME!

DEAR ME

start fresh,
start somewhere,
start somehow,
start something,
you are here,
be present,
look outside,
look inside.
it's YOU,
it's always been you.
the magic,
the spark,
that you are looking for.

A VERSION

Meeting you,
lead me to loving myself
Meeting you,
made me understand,
Meeting you,
means I am always the love
I always dream of.
I am that PERSON,
a different future version.

RAILROAD

my life wasn't easy,
If I told you today,
What I went through,
you could have wondered,
How did she survived that?
But I did and I'm here,
Somehow, I thought it'll end
to comfort me of not feeling the pain
and yet you got stuck of living.
A railroad of sadness and joy.

RAILROAD, yield

Little did you know,
you outgrew,
the old you,
it made you softer,
it made you bolder,
it made you calm,
I guess when you're
always surviving,
joy comes an unknown teritory
whilst chaos has become
your norm.

PARADOX

Is what I'm chasing?
Chasing me!
Happiness
seems to haunt me.
Sadness
seems to engulf me.
Chaos
seems to be always with me.
Calmness
seems to be an act to pursue.
If I sit,
can my life run on it's own?

REGRETS

I forgot
how to love,
I forgot to
say I care,
I forgot
about YOU.

PIECE

it's not easy
grieving
for that
person
you love
most
the person
who love me
unconditionally.
the person
whom I can be
and knows my quirks
You died,Dad
but you forgot
a part of me
died with you too.

VOID

I'm at loss
loss of words,
loss of thoughts,
loss of feelings,
even in void
a chaos,
broiling.
sighing in
silence
seems to be
an effort
I need to do.

HEARTBREAK

Does it ever stops?
the breaking,
the excruciating pain,
the guilt,
of feeling alive
when he's not.
Everyday,
I keep reminding myself
why you?
why not me?
why them?
why not you?

PLEA

I want you!
Please! Come back.
A plea
I desperately pray for
but
I can't
and
you can't
So
I'm left
with a memory
of
you

HOPE

I was breaking
but I was healing,
I was complaining
but I was expressing.
I want to escape
but I stayed in isolation.
I was kneeling
but it was Me, praying!
I thought
it was only me,
but you showed me
comfort in silence.

INSPIRATION

a little bit of joy
when I remember you,
a little bit of happiness,
when i see you smile.
a litte bit of gratefulness
when I know
you're proud of
where I am.

CHANGE

Change me,
but don't
change my heart
It has always been my weakness
and my strength.

A THOUGHT

Give
your
thought.
A
little
thought.

About the Author

A resident of Peace River,Alberta, Canada. A simple girl with an enormous love for poems and reading books, novels and etc. I am a registered nurse with experience of being a creative writer during my college days. I am also a Masters degree holder of Business Administration in Healthcare and Management in UCAM (Universidad Católica San Antonio de Murcia & Westford College). I am also a graduate of the Personal Support Worker Program in Sault College of Applied Arts and Technology.